AVI SHULMAN

Vitamins FOR THE Spirit

© *Copyright 2000 by* Shaar Press

First edition – First impression / March 2000

Published by **SHAAR PRESS**
Distributed by MESORAH PUBLICATIONS, LTD. .
4401 Second Avenue / Brooklyn, N.Y 11232 / (718) 921-9000
www.artscroll.com

ALL RIGHTS RESERVED

No part of this book may be reproduced **in any form,** *photocopy, electronic media, or otherwise without* **written** *permission from the copyright holder, except by a reviewer who wishes to quote brief passages in connection with a review written for inclusion in magazines or newspapers.*
THE RIGHTS OF THE COPYRIGHT HOLDER WILL BE STRICTLY ENFORCED.

ISBN: 1-57819-479-2 Paperback

Printed in the United States of America by Noble Book Press

This book is lovingly dedicated to my
brother-in-law and sister-in-law

Chatzkel and Liesel Merzel

Jerusalem, Israel

on the occasion of their

50th Anniversary

18 Kislev, 5760
November 27, 1999

They have been the guiding light of our family.
They have taught us how to honor parents, how to love
children and grandchildren, how to do meaningful
chesed, the joy of honest industry, how to integrate
Torah values into daily life, and how to love
Eretz Yisrael.

Every member of the family will
forever be grateful to
Uncle Chatzkel and Tanta Liesel
for the *zechus* of being part of their family.

May Hashem grant you many healthy, happy years of *nachas*
surrounded by your children, grandchildren, and great
grandchildren in Yerushalayim, and may you merit to be
at the coming of Moshiach.

Avi Shulman
Monsey, N.Y.

Table of Contents

	Thank you …	13
	Introduction	17
1.	When You Work on Your Goals … Your Goals Work on You	21
2.	The Hallmark of Maturity Is Taking Responsibility	23
3.	The Cynic Knows the Price of Everything … and the Value of Nothing	26
4.	Home Is the Place Where a Child Should Always Feel Best About Himself … and Comfortable Enough to Bring His Friends	28
5.	Everything Worthwhile Carries a Price Tag That Seems Too High	31
6.	Flood your Life With Ideas	33
7.	Burnout? Most People Haven't Even Been Lit Yet!	35
8.	Learn to Enjoy Taking Out the Garbage	37
9.	The Greatest Gift You Can Give a Child Is to See Him not as He Is, but as He Could Be and Help Him Get There	39
10.	Your Success in Life Will Be in Direct Proportion to What You Do Over and Above What Your Job Requires of You	41
11.	People Have Enough to Live on and Nothing to Live for	43
12.	Always Write a Name Next to a Phone Number	45
13.	Never Argue With a Fool in Public. People May Not Know Who the Real Fool Is.	47

14.	Be a Fountain of Inspiration	49
15.	Leave Everyone Feeling Better About Himself	51
16.	Learn to Swim Before You Learn to Sail	53
17.	You Will Never Feel Good by Making Excuses	55
18.	Teach Yourself to See the Rose, not the Thorn	57
19.	Make Many Mistakes, but Never the Same One Twice.	59
20.	Anything Worth Doing Is Worth Doing Poorly Until You Learn How to Do It Well	62
21.	Invest Two Percent of Your Income in Personal Growth	64
22.	Do Not Let the Perfect Spoil the Good	66
23.	If You Know How to Worry, You Are a Creative Thinker	68
24.	Most People Do Not Have Written Goals. Why? Because Without a Written Goal You Can't Fail.	70
25.	Are You Following the Followers?	72
26.	Until You Know Its Value, It Is Worthless!	75
27.	Expedient Routine Places Success Within Anyone's Grasp	76
28.	Photocopy the Contents of Your Wallet, and File the Copy	78
29.	Wear Out — Don't Rust Out!	80
30.	Never Walk on Anyone Else's Grass Regardless of Who Else Does!	82
31.	Never Invest in Anything You Don't Understand	84
32.	Great Goals Are Like Magnets	86
33.	It's NOT Fair!	88
34.	The More You Do "What You're Doing," the More You Will Get the Same as You Are Getting	90

35.	To Be Successful You Don't Have to Do Extraordinary Things ... Just Do Ordinary Things Extraordinarily Well!	92
36.	What You Think of Me, I'll Think of Me. And What I Think of Me, I'll Be.	94
37.	Failure Is Often the Result of a Lack of Information on How to Succeed	96
38.	The Fruit of Haste Is Regret	98
39.	There Are No Such Things as Opportunities Without Problems ... or Problems Without Opportunities	101
40.	You Wouldn't Be So Concerned About "What They Really Think About You" if You Realized How Seldom They Do	103
41.	You Don't Fail When You Fall Unless You Fail to Get Up	105
42.	Don't Worry About What Is Ahead — Just Go as Far as You Can See Now, and From There You Will Be Able to See Further	107
43.	Man Counts the Seeds of a Fruit. The A-mighty Counts the Fruit of a Seed	109
44.	We Don't See Things as They Are. We See Things as We Are.	111
45.	We Judge Others by Their Actions, but We Want Others to Judge Us by Our Intentions	113
46.	Most of the Trouble in the World is Caused by People Who Want to Be Important	115
47.	My Most Embarrassing Moments Occur When I Am Talking Instead of Listening	117
48.	The Joy of Your Excellent Proofreading Will Last Long After Your Speed Has Been Forgotten	118

49.	Courage Is Going From Failure to Failure With Enthusiasm	120
50.	A Person's Enthusiasm Stands in Direct Proportion to What He Is Looking Forward to	122
51.	People Form Habits … And Then Habits Form People.	124
52.	Life Has Not Taken a Hold of You Until You Begin Doing Things That the Average Person Considers Impossible.	126
53.	It Is Easier for Most People to Adjust Themselves to the Hardships Involved in Making a Poor Living Than to Adjust Themselves to the Hardships Involved in Making Their Lives Better	128
54.	Never Be a Slave to the Tyranny of the Urgent.	130
55.	To Be Successful We Don't Have to Find Something New; We Need Only to Find Ways of Doing Old Things Better	132
56.	If Excellence Is My Goal, Then Criticism Is My Ally	134
57.	Don't Depend on Anyone Else for Your Happiness, Your Fulfillment, or for Your Growth	137
58.	For the Person Who Is Willing to Serve Before Trying to Collect … There Are Abundant Opportunities	139
59.	A Great Deal of Talent Is Lost to the world for Want of Courage. Talent Resides in Action.	141
60.	People Grow Old by Deserting Their Ideals	143
61.	Be Happy With What You Have While in Pursuit of What You Want	145
62.	What I Am to Be, I Am Now Becoming	147
63.	Healthy Relationships Are Usually Sweet-tempered	148

64.	Did You Do Your Best? If Not, Why Not?	150
65.	Perhaps My Life's Challenge Is to Be Humble Even When I'm Right (to Compensate for My Being Arrogant When I Am Wrong)	151
66.	The Power of Three-word Phrases	153
67.	The Mistake We Often Make Is That We Stop Working on Ourselves as Soon as We Are Doing Better.	158
68.	If You Don't Appreciate Your Strengths, You Can't Eliminate Your Weaknesses	160
69.	What You Take For Granted, Your Children Don't Even Know	162
70.	What You Consider a Well-deserved Luxury, Your Children Deem a Necessity	164
71.	Don't Buy a "Bargain In Reverse"	167
72.	Don't Write ... Rewrite	169
73.	Success Principle: Under-promise and Over-deliver	171
74.	Don't Ask, "What Will I Get?" Rather Ask, "What Will I Become?"	172
75.	Success Comes to Those Who Refuse to Fail	174
76.	There Is No Glory in the *Preparation* to Win, but You Can't Have The Glory of the "Win" Without the Preparation.	176
77.	I Don't Eat Junk Food Because I Need My Body to Perform at Its Best so That I Can Perform at My Best	178
78.	There Is No Sadder Sight Than a Young Pessimist	180
79.	You Steer a Sailboat by Adjusting Its Rudders	181
80.	Most of the Progress Made by A Sailboat Is Against the Wind	183

81.	The Effectiveness of a Sailboat Is in the Coordination of the Sail and the Rudder	185
82.	Although There Is Never Enough Time to Do Everything, There Is Always Enough Time to Do the Most Important Thing — and To Stay With It Until It Is Done *Right*	187
83.	Don't Just Go Through Life: Grow Through It!	189
84.	Ask for Help — not Because You Are — Weak, but Because You Want to Remain Strong	190
85.	Until the Pain of Staying the Same Is Greater Than the Pain of Change, We Will Never Change	192
86.	Refusing to Accept Things as They Are Is What Drives A Person To Great Accomplishments	194
87.	On the Average, Each Person Will Experience (Either He Himself or Someone Close To Him) Several Major Tragedies	196
88.	Problems: Either You Just Left One, or You Are in One, or You Are Headed Toward One	197
89.	Just When Tou See the Light at the End of the Tunnel, They Add More Tunnel	199
90.	No Blame No Excuses No Complaints No Self-pity.	200
91.	If You're Not Actively Involved in Getting What You Want, You Don't Really Want It Enough	202
92.	A Wise Man Demands of Himself What a Fool Demands of Others	203
93.	A Wise Man Learns From His Mistakes. A Wiser Man Learns From Mistakes Made by Others.	204

Thank You ...

First, I wish to express profound gratitude to Hashem for having given me so much in the way of life, health, talents, opportunities, a very special family, friends, and community. I am especially blessed to have always been associated with *bnei Torah* and Torah personalities.

My father's *zt"l yiras Shamayim*, integrity, and dedication to Torah have been constant inspirations to me. No doubt, the benevolence Hashem has shown me is a result of *zechus avos*.

I want to express appreciation to the very special people who over the last several years have embraced me with concern, support, and true friendship. Each, in his own way and at the right time, has helped and inspired me. In many ways, this book is the product of what I have learned from them.

My family — my wife Erica, our children, and their extended families. All of you individually and as a group have helped us through difficult times.

My Torah Umesorah family — with special appreciation to Rabbi Joshua Fishman, and *my "Seed" family* with special appreciation to Rabbi Joseph Grunfeld of London.

My Mercaz family — with special appreciation to Rabbis Wein and Joel Kramer.

My ArtScroll family, my Beis Shraga family,

my Yeshivah of Spring Valley family, my rebbes and my chavrusos, all my good friends, my "boys club," with special appreciation to Reb Shlomo Stern.

To all of you, a tremendous "Thank you."

INTRODUCTION

An aphorism is a condensed truism. It is a statement that captures the essence of a whole lesson in just a few words.

Think of vitamin C. We usually obtain it from fresh fruits and vegetables, and when we eat enough of these we get an adequate dose of this vitamin.

However, when you don't have the time to eat all the fruits and vegetables you need, when they are not available, or when your body needs an extra dose of vitamins, a vitamin pill is the way to quickly provide your body with all the vitamins it needs, including vitamin C.

There are important life lessons all around us if we have the time, patience, and insight to learn them. Not all of us have these; therefore, this small book of aphorisms and insights may serve as a much-needed vitamin pill.

I found these "words of wisdom" especially effective at the beginning of a class — to stimulate the thinking process (and to get the students to appreciate even the first few minutes of class).

I was amazed to see that when I taught these aphorisms in class, some adult students often didn't fully appreciate the "insight" or lesson value until I explained it to them. However, when I did clarify it, they greatly appreciated the new understanding.

Accordingly, I was gratified when Rabbi Meir Zlotowitz suggested that I publish these aphorisms and their explanations.

I believe that every father and mother should leave to their children and grandchildren a "treasury of important life lessons," a legacy of life-skills. These will include ideas, insights, and lessons that they accumulated from *sefarim*, books, lectures, observations, and personal life experiences. Since parents want only the best for their children, why must each child go through the "college of hard knocks" himself to learn what his parents have learned and can teach him from experience?

This small book contains just such lessons in the area of practical life-skills. I sincerely hope that my own children and grandchildren will learn from it, and I am gratified to share it with both my students and readers.

There are two observations:

(1) I have collected these various statements over 30 years. Some of them I originated, while many reflect the thinking of others, but I can't recall who they are; therefore I don't mention anyone by name. The explanations, however, are mine, and I thus take full responsibility for them.

(2) I offer these as useful "conversation starters" for parents to use in priming the pump of conversation with their children. Please don't present these as absolute truths; rather, consider them as handy starting points for good conversations.

I would like to thank Rabbis Meir Zlotowitz and Nosson Scherman (who personally read and corrected every page), both lifelong friends, and Reb Sheah Brander. All of us owe them a tremendous debt of gratitude, because they have provided us with insights into *Tefillah*, *Tanach*, Talmud and Jewish history and thought, that have greatly enhanced everyone's learning opportunities.

Rabbi Hillel L. Yarmove and Mrs. Judi Dick edited the manuscript and added their considerable personal flair to the work. For reading and helping prepare this book, I am especially grateful to Rabbi and Mrs. Yisroel Flam, Mordechai Shulman, Mrs. Brocha Scheinberg, Mrs. Malka Goldberg, and my wife, Erica.

Avi Shulman

Monsey, New York
Adar Sheni 5760
March 2000

WHEN YOU WORK ON YOUR GOALS ... YOUR GOALS WORK ON YOU

There are two separate and distinct benefits in setting and achieving a goal. The first benefit is the achievement of the goal itself. For example, you set out to write a book. You research the material, gather information, speak to experts, structure all the material, write it, have it proofread, set in type, printed, and distributed. The book you now proudly hold in your hands is the fruition of the original goal, the concrete manifestation of the transformation of an idea and a dream into reality. The benefits are obvious.

There is a second, less-overt benefit in working on a goal, and that is what you become on the way to achieving it. When you research the information, you become an expert on the subject; when you interview experts, you rub shoulders with the elite of that field; when you structure the information, you develop clarity and the ability to present the material in logical sequence.

The first benefit — the completion of the book — is dramatic: You can physically hold the book in your hands; you can actually show it to someone. It calls out and says, "You did it!"

The second benefit is less dramatic — but important despite being more subtle. If writing a book was your goal, then even if you went through all the steps but for some reason the book was not published, you have become more knowledgeable, an eminent expert in your chosen field in the process. Indeed, when you work on your goals, your goals work on you.

THE HALLMARK OF MATURITY IS TAKING RESPONSIBILITY

Taking responsibility very often hurts: It is so much easier to say it's not my fault.

Listen to a two- or three-year-old child explain why the table is covered with milk. "The milk spilled." He should have said, "I spilled the milk," but instead he said it spilled. Who spilled it? He doesn't know, nor does it even matter to him: He didn't do it.

Maturity begins with the statement, "I spilled the milk." However, the person who hides behind "but it wasn't my fault because … " is only halfway there. Full maturity comes when we're big enough to say, "I did it; it was my fault, and I take full responsibility!" When you can face up to the realization that it was you who did it, you are responsible! You can now begin to initiate improvement.

Not too long ago, I read two lists of actual excuses students gave for not doing their homework. The first list was written 30 years ago. The second list is more recent.

Excuses Then:
- Homework?
- My dog ate it.
- It's at home.
- I lost it.
- I forgot to take the book home.
- I thought it was optional.
- I didn't hear the assignment.

Excuses Now:
- My computer has a virus.
- I faxed it to you. Didn't you get it?
- The assignment isn't politically correct.
- Are you harassing me?
- I want to plea bargain.
- The assignment discriminates against boys, girls, etc.

The bottom line of both lists: It's not my fault!

THE CYNIC KNOWS THE PRICE OF EVERYTHING ... AND THE VALUE OF NOTHING

The cynic sits in a very comfortable position: He contributes nothing and risks nothing, yet he takes potshots at anyone at will.

Cynicism also has this aspect: It is indirect rather than direct. A child who comes late and is asked, "Why are you late?" has the opportunity of answering the question forthrightly. If, however, a parent sarcastically says to that child, "I'm happy to see that you came early again," the child, who is the target, cannot respond to the attack.

Chazal say that one cynical word — turning something serious into a joke — can refute 100 admonitions. This is truly amazing! Imagine that someone presents to an audience a well-thought-out reason to do something, then a second reason, then a third, and on and on until we have 100 logical reasons. We're all moved to take action! Then one wise guy makes a cynical crack ("e.g., the speaker probably has a vested interest"), and all 100 reasons just melt away!

Such is the power of cynicism!

Home Is the Place Where a Child Should Always Feel Best About Himself ... and Comfortable Enough to Bring His Friends

Where do you dock a boat? We might imagine that the easiest place would be to dock a boat on a pier directly alongside the ocean. The boat would thus have easy access both to and from the port.

In practice, however, that's not where boats are docked. They are docked in a safe harbor. A safe harbor is a protected inlet of water enclosed on three sides by natural barriers or by man-made sea walls. The narrow opening into the safe harbor allows boats to enter, but keeps out rough winds and waves. The safe harbor is a calm and tranquil area that protects the boat from harsh ocean waves.

A boat can travel for days or weeks with its crew on 24-hour alert. At any time it can be buffeted by high winds, gales, and storms that can damage or even sink it. But the minute the boat enters a safe harbor, all concerns of the captain and crew are over. Here the boat floats safely, out of harm's way.

That's a pretty accurate description of how a child should feel when he opens the door to his home. The teacher may have insinuated that his work is less than desirable, a grade on a test may seem a harsh indictment, his friends may have mocked something he feels strongly about — but all of these less-than-thrilling experiences disappear the moment he opens the front door. Home is a safe harbor. Home is where he doesn't have to be afraid of criticism, sarcasm, or an attack on his self-esteem.

Most important, home should be a place where a child feels comfortable to bring his friends, knowing that he will never be reprimanded in front of them. Notwithstanding the good intentions of parents, the child who is embarrassed in front of his peers could be deeply hurt. The incident might be remembered for years; the damage may last for decades.

EVERYTHING WORTHWHILE CARRIES A PRICE TAG THAT SEEMS TOO HIGH

A story is told about a great violinist who had just completed playing a most beautiful concerto when a woman ran over to him and gushed, "Maestro, I'd give *anything* to play like that!"

He looked at her for what seemed to be a long time. His thoughts must have spanned the decades. Finally he said, "That's just what I did."

The price for his great mastery of the violin

was years replete with six, eight, and 10 hours each day spent practicing; single-minded dedication; forgoing the pleasures and social activities of his youth; and deprivation — all of these were the "price" of achieving something worthwhile.

When we say "price" we refer to the cost of acquisition, whether in terms of physical, mental, or emotional duress.

The opposite of paying a high price for something worthwhile is to pay little for something that is almost valueless. In almost every area of life, the bargain is usually the more expensive choice.

FLOOD YOUR LIFE WITH IDEAS

It has been said, "What I am to be, I am now becoming," which means simply that if in the future I want to be _____ (you fill in the blank), the preparation for that achievement has to start some time in advance, preferably now.

One of the best ways to grow is to flood your life with ideas.

If a baker wants to bake a cake but the ingredients available to him are limited to just a few products, the choice of cakes would be extremely limited. On the other hand, a baker who has a pantry full of ingredients could bake almost any cake he desires, suitable for the guest and the occasion.

Ideas are ingredients with which we build our thoughts. The more ideas we have, the more varied the choices open to us — and the richer these choices will be.

Burnout? Most People Haven't Even Been Lit Yet!

Burnout is often the result of perceiving your work as uninteresting, uninspiring, and monotonous. The truth is that even in the most pedestrian and mundane work — such as cleaning your office or your home — you can find ways of working that are challenging and rewarding.

I once spoke to a man who worked his way through college by cleaning houses. After graduating, he sought work in his new profession when he realized that he had greater opportunities to establish a following in the home- and office-cleaning business. In a short time he built the largest cleaning service in an 11-state region. He then began giving demonstrations to women's groups on the ways to clean a home most efficiently. He subsequently became a well-known public speaker and authored over a dozen books on these and related subjects.

It has been said that there is no such thing as a boring job, just boring people.

LEARN TO ENJOY TAKING OUT THE GARBAGE

The imagery which draws young men and women to marriage is the joy of a festive holiday table, companionship, family, and the like — but not a vision of taking out the garbage, cleaning house, or changing diapers.

But the fact is that if the garbage were not taken out, the house not cleaned, or the diapers not changed, the marriage wouldn't work!

Thus, taking out the garbage (and doing all those other necessary but unpleasant tasks) is as important to the full-functioning family and household as are the pleasant events. When we understand this, we can tolerate and even learn to enjoy doing unpleasant tasks.

THE GREATEST GIFT YOU CAN GIVE A CHILD IS TO SEE HIM NOT AS HE IS, BUT AS HE COULD BE — AND HELP HIM GET THERE

If this were the watchword of every home and every classroom, the world would be a better place.

When guests arrive, one parent whom I know introduces each of his children in a wonderful way: "This young lady is Russie. Although she is only 9 years old, in many ways she is grown up. On Shabbos, Russie comes early to shul and *davens* nearly the whole *davening*. We see a beautiful young lady growing up!"

Quite an improvement over "this is Russie!"

When eating in a restaurant and being approached by a waiter, parents should say, "Each of our children has very good taste; please treat him or her as an adult." Even if the parent then feels the need to modify an inappropriate choice, such a blooper is insignificant, since his parents' opinion of him is so very positive!

At a Torah Umesorah convention Rav Pam said that when he was 15 years old, his rebbi, Rabbi David Leibowitz, would address him as "*ihr*" (a sign of respect, as opposed to "*du*"). Years later, Rav Pam still recalled the thrill and motivation of being so addressed.

Your Success in Life Will Be in Direct Proportion to What You Do Over and Above What Your Job Requires of You

Read the biographies of people who have achieved, and you'll find a common thread that weaves its way through their lives.

They have done more than they had to — and more than they were paid for.

The student who studies more than what was minimally required of him, the salesman who expresses interest in his customer's welfare beyond the scope of the "sale," the professional who researches unrelated but important subjects in addition to those serving his customer's needs, and the executive who invests extra time in developing new markets — are all examples of people who do over and above what their jobs require.

There is hardly a person who became outstanding in his chosen field by doing *just* what was required — and no more!

You can't become above-average by performing average deeds.

People Have Enough to Live on and Nothing to Live for

At one time the overriding concern of people worldwide was having adequate food, clothing, and shelter "to live."

Today most people in the Western world have enough to live on, yet they struggle with the fundamental question — what to "live for." A good income provides lots of free time and opportunities, but only a thinking person can decide what to do with his time and which options to seize. These choices tell us more than anything else what sort of person he or she is.

To most of the world "philosophy" implies a useless exercise of words and thoughts that doesn't lead anywhere, or, better stated — doesn't affect us at all. Yet each of us develops a "philosophy of life" which represents the purpose of life. The more clearly that purpose is understood and the greater clarity with which it is expressed, the more our lives will be enriched.

Always Write a Name Next to a Phone Number

Have you ever written a phone number on a scrap of paper and have no idea whose number it is? Or more embarrassing, you dialed a number thinking that you were going to speak to one person and found that instead you were speaking to someone else — possibly someone to whom you might not have wanted to speak?

Hopefully, this doesn't happen too often, but here is a simple trick you can teach yourself to start a habit that will serve you well: Always write a name next to a phone number.

There are two immediate benefits:

(1) You'll always know whom you are calling, and

(2) You will have retrained yourself to acquire a new habit.

There are many people who live by the credo, "You can't teach an old dog new tricks." They say it so often that they probably have convinced themselves of it. But we believe that people are not dogs and that education is not "tricks." We believe that an intelligent person can retrain himself/herself to acquire good habits in every area of life.

Every time you practice a new behavior until it becomes an automatic action, you are developing a habit and you are thereby reinforcing this wholesome, healthy behavior. Writing a name next to a phone number — actually creating a new habit — becomes a big deal. It reinforces your ability to acquire new habits.

That's the way to go; that's the way to grow!

Never Argue With a Fool in Public. People May Not Know Who the Real Fool Is.

Arguing with a fool any time any place is not a good practice, but arguing with a fool in public is an absolutely no-win situation. The irony is that regardless of how absurd the fool's argument is, you will always find people who will agree with him. Before long you may even find yourself wondering who is the fool.

We are taught (*Proverbs* 26:4): "Do not answer a fool according to *his* folly." Even when we must argue with a fool, the argument should never descend to his level. He may raise his voice, toss out insults, and use foul language. Don't sink to his level.

BE A FOUNTAIN OF INSPIRATION

Inspiration makes all the difference.

An inspired student, even one with modest abilities, will eventually outperform an uninspired talented student.

An inspired salesman will sell his product in spite of difficulties.

An inspired mother will create an atmosphere of hope even in the most dire circumstances.

Yet, as potent a force as inspiration is, many of us do not see it as a trait that can be acquired. We fool ourselves into believing that some people are "inspired" and others are "not inspired," just as some people are tall and others are short. We mistakenly believe that we too were born inspired or uninspired and cannot change. The truth is that anyone can learn to "become inspired" and then become an inspired parent or teacher.

We can become inspired people by surrounding ourselves exclusively with positive and inspirational people, and by reading materials, and listening to cassettes that are positive and motivational. Fill your mind with faith, hope and success; learn to see the potential and the accomplishments of man; and in time these will become part of your thinking process. Suddenly, you are an "inspired person"!

It makes a world of difference!

LEAVE EVERYONE FEELING BETTER ABOUT HIMSELF

"I feel better about myself when I'm with you" has to be one of the all-time great compliments. Of all the gifts we can give a friend — flowers, books, jewelry, clothing, or a trip — none rivals the gift of the basic good feeling which a person needs to have about himself.

When you can tap into that need, when you have learned and acquired the skill of making the time you spend with someone a constructive experience, you have become a very special friend.

People will go to extreme lengths to find someone who will honestly make them feel better about themselves. Please note that the crucial word is "honestly," because only if such a feeling is *honestly and sincerely* instilled in a person does it become meaningful.

Learn to Swim Before You Learn to Sail

Sometimes even the simplest, most obvious truths escape us. We find ourselves taking the second step before the first just because we haven't thought through the process.

Many people who want to paint a room begin by opening a can of paint and painting. When they are faced with things such as light fixtures, they remove them (with paint-stained hands), cover the furniture (only after some paint has already dripped on it), and take out the chairs (with dirty hands).

Watch a professional painter prepare a room. Before he even opens a paint can, he will move small items, carefully cover furniture with a drop cloth, tape the corners of windows, remove all electric fixtures, switch plates, and the like. He can spend hours in preparation because experience has taught him that the time invested in preparing is well worth it.

The time we invest in planning is indeed manifoldly repaid.

You Will Never Feel Good by Making Excuses

All that "making good excuses" proves is that you know how to make good excuses.

But not being in class — even with the best excuse — still leaves you without the knowledge imparted that day; being late for a meeting — even with the best excuse — still leaves you at a disadvantage; missing making a sale — even with a great excuse — still leaves you without the income.

Of course, there are times when with good

reason, you have to miss class, come late to a meeting, or miss a sale.

But don't — in your own mind — perceive the "good excuse" as the fulfillment of the missed opportunity.

Excuses may allow us to get by and enable us to survive, but they will never allow us to thrive.

"Feeling good" results only from doing worthwhile things.

TEACH YOURSELF TO SEE THE ROSE, NOT THE THORN

Every rose has both a beautiful flower and a stem full of thorns. We have to teach ourselves consciously to see, admire, appreciate, and remember the spectacular colors and aroma of the rose and not to concentrate on the thorns.

This may seem simple — even superfluous — to say, yet so many people's lives and memories are caught up in the "thorns" of life.

Every situation has its flower and its thorns. The thorns are real, and they can prick, puncture, hurt, and cause one to bleed; but the purpose of the rose is its flower, not its thorns. It is our choice to see what we wish to see. (Perhaps the thorns are there to make sure that we appreciate the flower by contrast!)

Teach yourself to be aware of the thorn and not let it snag you, but respond to and remember only the flower.

MAKE MANY MISTAKES, BUT NEVER THE SAME ONE TWICE

We learn by making mistakes if (and this is really the big *if*):

(1) We see making mistakes as part of the natural learning process.

(2) We do not see mistakes as depreciating us as human beings.

(3) We learn from our mistakes and don't repeat them.

It is hard to imagine a child learning how to

walk without falling down, or an adult learning new skills without making mistakes.

- Learning to play tennis means missing many balls.
- Learning a new subject means not understanding it at first.
- Learning how to bake a new cake means risking an inedible glob.
- Learning how to drive can mean making turns too sharply and stopping too abruptly.

When you internalize the concept that all growth comes with the risk of failing but that failure is part and parcel of growth, you will have taken one giant step toward personal growth.

The second step — learning from your mistakes — is also a giant step: You must analyze these mistakes and take constructive steps to prevent them from recurring. For example:

- You invest based on a hot tip and lose your hard-earned money. The mistake is not in "the market" but rather in the misinformation or lack of research on which you made your investment.

- You direct an amateur performance, and some things inevitably go wrong. After the event the real challenge is to immediately analyze what went wrong and why. Think of better ways to direct a play next time, immediately write down your ideas, and at the next time opportunity follow them.

- You speak in public and don't do well. The answer is not to say, "Public speaking is not for me," and run away from ever doing it again, but rather to find out what you did wrong and how you can correct it.

When you take these simple steps you will have great tools for growing.

Anything Worth Doing Is Worth Doing Poorly Until You Learn How to Do It Well

I once heard a parent admonish a child for doing something wrong and scream, "I don't want you ever to do anything until you know how to do it right."

To this day I wonder how that child was ever expected to learn to do anything new if he was never afforded the opportunity to do it poorly at first and then to eventually learn to do it well.

Watching a child (or, for that matter, an adult) do something wrong as he learns to do it correctly takes patience and the ability to refrain from comment and criticism.

Self-control and discipline on the part of the parent will go a long way toward building the child's self-confidence and "risk-taking" ability.

Invest Two Percent of Your Income in Personal Growth

Few enterprises would stay in business if they did not invest money each year in R & D — research and development. "Research and development" does not mean that the business has a problem which threatens its future existence. It may actually be doing very well marketing its current products.

Nevertheless, since management knows well that its future depends on the new products or methods it develops today, it is willing — or, more precisely, eager — to invest heavily in future growth.

A person is no different. If in the next few years he does only what he is doing now, he has little chance of growth.

Set aside two percent of your income each year for personal growth in the form of books, cassettes, and development programs. By setting aside a "special growth fund for this purpose," you won't hesitate to spend the necessary money when the opportunity to acquire these items arises.

Do Not Let the Perfect Spoil the Good

"Perfect" is in many situations an unrealistic goal.

Do you know what a "perfect" batting average is? It is 1,000 percent. To achieve such an average, a player must get a hit every time he is at bat, but in real life even a .300 average is considered good. A consistent .333 average, hitting one out of three, and missing two out of the three, would earn the batter champion status. Even that rare .400 hitter is out three of every five times he comes to bat!

In golf a "perfect" score is 18 — a hole-in-one for each hole — yet many excellent players have never had even one hole-in-one throughout their entire careers. A score of 80 is considered good, and a 70 marks one as being of championship caliber.

What can the unrealistic expectation of perfection do to the baseball player or golfer? It can so frustrate him that he loses concentration, enjoyment, and even the will to play!

Very similar is our expectation of perfection in many areas of our lives. We can strive for perfection just as the batter strives for a hit each time at bat, but we must not allow the illusion of perfection to spoil our "good work."

The upshot: Always try to improve in everything you do, but *don't let the perfect spoil the good.*

IF YOU KNOW HOW TO WORRY, YOU ARE A CREATIVE THINKER

Do you have a creative imagination? If you know how to worry, then you do.

People say they are not creative. Yet, worry is a great exercise in creative thinking, albeit negative creative thinking.

Here is how the thinking process goes. "If I don't make the sale, my boss will be angry with me, and he may decide to review my last six months performance. Measured against some of the super salesman, I may look bad ... he may fire me ... I won't be able to find another job ... I'll depreciate my savings ... get behind in my mortgage ... have to sell the house ... go on welfare ...

A great example of negative creative thinking. This scenario takes imagination, creativity, and the stringing together of hypothetical situations.

If we can "worry" we have the tools to use positive creative imagery. We can learn how to use the same thought process to develop a "good scenario."

Most People Do Not Have Written Goals. Why? Because Without a Written Goal You Can't Fail!

I never understood why people resist writing down their goals. Every book on "getting things done" states a simple truth: Those who have goals (and written goals seem to be the only kind that really count) have a greater chance of succeeding than those who don't.

The success books say so, the management courses say so, and the vast majority of achievers will tell you that rule one is to draw up goals and put them in writing.

Yet only three percent of the population have written goals.

A person begins a project — to learn a subject, acquire a skill, or even lose some weight — and he thinks to himself, "How long will this project take?" If he sets a time by which to complete the project — say, in four weeks — and at the end of four weeks he has not met the requirements to finish the project, in a sense he has failed. However, if he leaves the question of "how long?" or "how much?" unanswered, *he can never fail!*

Even in our own minds, we are so afraid of failure that we would rather forgo the proven advantage of a tried-and-true process — in this case using written goals — than risk *imagined* failure.

Now that we understand that it is just the fear of *imagined* failure that is holding us back from writing down our goals, we can confront this fear head-on.

ARE YOU FOLLOWING THE FOLLOWERS?

As individuals, most people are reasonable. As a member of a crowd, the same people become blockheads.

Throughout recorded history, the majority of mankind has generally been wrong when it has followed the followers.

Although this is true in every discipline — for example, politics, medicine, religion, education, science, and art — the most obvious example is finance. Look at the following examples of this axiom:

Dutch Tulip Mania, 1600's

Mississippi Company — John Law, 1700's

South Sea Bubble, 1700's

Erie Railroad, 1850's (any company with the word "rail")

Anglo-American Electric Light Co. (any company with the word "electric")

Charles Ponzi, 1920's

Investors Overseas Service (IOS), 1970's

Michael Miliken (Drexel Burnham Lambert), 1980's

New Era Charity, 1990's

Viatical Settlements, 1997

_____

_____

_____

[The above has been left blank intentionally, for future — and as yet unknown — "great, unbelievable opportunities" which will belong on such a list.]

Every one of these "investments" in their time caused near-hysteria, as people virtually fell over themselves to invest (after all, everyone knows what a great investment this is …). The subsequent loss of millions of dollars is a classic example of what happens when people follow the followers.

Until You Know Its Value, It Is Worthless!

If you buy a sheet of tin for $10 and sell it for $11 and then discover that it really was a sheet of silver worth $1000, you have no valid claim that it was a mistake. You bought tin and you sold tin!

Think about all the things to which many people don't attribute real value until they are lost: health, happiness, family, friends, freedom — even gifts such as air, water, and sunshine.

Do yourself a favor: Learn to value these gifts even while you have them.

EXPEDIENT ROUTINE PLACES SUCCESS WITHIN ANYONE'S GRASP

Routine — which is really an organized set of habits — goes a long way toward helping one become successful. Even someone with "mediocre" talents can become successful in whatever area he chooses if he can but learn to follow a pattern of logical steps routinely.

The real challenge is to learn to make a habit of the very things that most people don't want to do.

Here are some simple examples:

- Getting up early
- Reading daily
- Listening to motivational cassettes
- Learning new vocabulary words daily
- Using commuting time wisely
- Practicing giving a speech
- Rereading a letter
- Training yourself to do a project before it's due
- Planning
- Writing down goals
- Not allowing distractions

We may even routinely be friendly and courteous to everyone we meet. This is what people mean when they say that "practice makes perfect."

Photocopy the Contents of Your Wallet, and File the Copy

The loss of a wallet or pocketbook is traumatic. In addition to your loss of money, driver's license, credit cards, and the like, there is also a feeling of being stripped of your identity.

You must also deal with the additional frustration of not knowing exactly what you had in your wallet.

Suggestion: Periodically (for example, every January 1 and July 1) photocopy everything in your wallet. File this copy so that in the event of loss or theft you'll know what you had, and the pertinent information on the copy will help you to replace the missing documents.

Wear Out — Don't Rust Out!

Visit the workshop of a master craftsman, and you will see tools that may be old but have been maintained with such loving care that they function as well as and often better than new ones. You'll see the craftsman use these tools and then carefully clean them, placing them in protective covers. Little wonder that they serve him well for decades.

Contrast this to someone who carelessly leaves his tools lying around. In just a few months the tools become rusty and unusable.

A person has the ability to care for himself or

to neglect himself — the difference between wearing out after a lifetime of fully productive years or merely rusting out.

Never Walk on Anyone's Grass Regardless of Who Else Does!

You may not mind when someone else walks on your grass, but there are people who take great pride in their lawns — and they do mind.

These people personally prepare the soil. They seed it and fertilize it, and once the grass has begun to sprout, they weed it, water it, and cut (almost manicure) it, putting in many hours of work and investing much money.

To these people, walking on their lawn is an abuse of something of great value.

The lesson here is that even though you don't take great pride in your lawn, someone else may take pride in his. You can't judge someone else's values by your own.

Just as this is true about a lawn, so is it true about everything else in life.

Rabbi Eliyahu Lopian said that the definition of "life" is what you can never get enough of. To some people life is music. To other people life is sports. To still others it is learning. Don't abuse someone else's "life."

NEVER INVEST IN ANYTHING YOU DON'T UNDERSTAND

There are three separate and important principles at work here:

Principle #1: You are capable of understanding investments.

Principle #2: If at present you don't understand investments, it is because you have not spent time reading and learning about them. In 25-50 hours (and in many cases, fewer) you can get a working knowledge of investments that should fit your needs.

Principle #3: If after you have read and studied you still don't understand enough about that particular investment, then that investment is not for you.

Tremendous amounts of money have been lost by people who could least afford such losses because they made investments that they didn't understand.

This principle applies as well to other areas of life.

Great Goals Are Like Magnets

Make sure the greatest pull on you is the "pull of the future."

One of life's greatest experiences is to work on a project that pulls you. A researcher working on a cure is "pulled" by the dream of discovery. The entrepreneur trying to introduce a new product and a student working toward a degree are both examples to which we can easily relate.

But the "pull" doesn't necessarily have to be as dramatic as in these cases. A businessman might be "pulling" to finish the year in the black, a mother might be "pulled" to help her children get ahead, or a person might be "pulled" to learn a new skill.

"Pull" and "future" go hand in hand.

Unfortunately, many people go through life with the "pull" of the past. "I should have" and "I could have" are all "pulls" of the past. People don't jump out of bed early in the morning very enthusiastically to take on a "pull" of the past. So make sure your "pull" is a future one.

The easiest way to hoist yourself up is by using a pulley. Make your future goal the pulley by which you lift yourself.

It's Not Fair!

The world is not fair. It really isn't.

My grandfather immigrated to America, leaving his whole family in Europe. All his siblings and their children (my uncles, aunts, and cousins) suffered hunger, deprivation, the ravages of war, and the Holocaust.

I didn't: It's not fair!

There are millions of illiterates who never will know the joy of a book or the pleasure of a letter. They are cut off from the world of thought.

I am not: It's not fair!

There are millions who go to sleep hungry every night.

I don't: It's not fair!

There are millions who don't have my health, wealth, family, or prestige.

I do: It's not fair!

If everything in the world were really fair, you, I, and everyone else in the world would have:

Food: Three slices of bread daily.
Clothing: One dress or one pair of pants.
Housing: One room for your whole family.
Phone: One phone shared by 200 families.
Car: One car shared by 500 families.

The very next time you hear someone (even yourself) say, "It's not fair!" ask, "Would you really be happy if *everything* were fair?"

THE MORE YOU DO "WHAT YOU'RE DOING," THE MORE YOU WILL GET THE SAME AS YOU ARE GETTING

If you want something to be different — if you want to change the way things are — then you can't keep doing things exactly as you are doing them now! This is a relatively simple concept.

There is a saying that only a fool thinks he can continue to do the same thing and get different results.

For instance, you see a parent yell at his child, who ignores him. The parent continues to yell and scream at the child, and the child continues to ignore him. Since the parent sees that this method doesn't work (he's not getting the desired results), why doesn't he consider changing the method?

A person tries to get ahead in business but doesn't. Yet he continues to do exactly what he has been doing over the years — to no avail.

Question: If you see that your methods are not working (you're not getting ahead), why not consider some new methods?

For the most part, people are so rigid in their ways — so set in the way they do things — that they would rather continue "doing what they've been doing" even when they continue to get negative results.

TO BE SUCCESSFUL YOU DON'T HAVE TO DO EXTRAORDINARY THINGS ... JUST DO ORDINARY THINGS EXTRAORDINARILY WELL!

When we hear of a person who has achieved unusual success, many of us have the tendency to discount it by saying, "That person has extraordinary talent."

In a way it makes us feel better because it answers the unasked question: "If that person is successful, why am I not successful, too?" By placing this person on a pedestal (he has unusual talents), we have justified our own position (because we *don't* have extraordinary talents).

The truth is that to be successful you don't have to do extraordinary things or to have any extraordinary talents. But you do need to set your mind to do even ordinary things *extraordinarily well*.

The teacher who prepares her lesson extraordinarily well, who prepares interesting and enjoyable workshops, who searches for ideas and stories to make his class come "alive" — in other words, doing ordinary things (teaching a class) in an extraordinary way — will be inordinately successful. In every field — homemaking, the professions, business — the same is true; you can take seemingly ordinary tasks and inject them with creative thinking, enthusiasm, and loving care — and you will be successful.

What You Think of Me, I'll Think of Me. And What I Think of Me, I'll Be.

The small child really doesn't know his own strengths or weaknesses until someone tells them to him.

Parents, teachers, classmates, and friends have a tremendous impact on the young child's self image because, to a large extent, he will trust their evaluation — and try to live up to it.

The parent who constantly compliments the child on his polite manners is saying to the child, "That is what I think of you — you're a polite, well-mannered child." And in most cases the child will live up to his parents' appraisal.

The teacher who compliments the student on her work habits says to the student, "I think you work very proficiently …," and the student buys into that thinking and tries to live up to it.

What you think of me, I'll be.

Failure Is Often the Result of a Lack of Information on How to Succeed

Do you know that there is information available on "succeeding" in any given field. Information can be found in the form of books, articles, cassettes, classes, or people well-versed in that area. But in almost every area, there is a mountain of information available only if we are ready to search for it.

People have the tendency to jump into situations without wanting to do the research, because doing research — really studying, finding out, listening to experts, and taking notes — is boring in comparison to actually beginning and doing the project!

Don't let that fool you. Research pays off. It leads to success.

THE FRUIT OF HASTE IS REGRET

In this one brief six-word phrase we are taught an enormous lesson about successful human relationships.

Haste in answering a question, haste in making a business decision, haste in making a judgment, haste in responding to a perceived insult — all these have done immeasurable harm to families, friends, and business associates.

For example, in public-speaking class we are taught that when you are asked a question following a lecture, even if you have the right

answer on the tip of your tongue, don't respond as soon as the question is asked! Here is how you should answer a question:
- Listen to the question.
- Wait five seconds (mentally count 1-2-3-4-5).
- Now answer the question.

The five seconds that you have waited may seem like a small amount of time, but even seconds will go a long way toward preventing you from blurting out a foolish remark. There is no reason why you can't ask for more time to think. You can say, "I need a few minutes more to think about that." If the question warrants a longer period of time, ask for a few days.

The regrets of a hastily spoken word or act can last for years, decades, and, in some cases, a lifetime.

In school we were taught that being first with the answer to a question is a sign of being "sharp" and "bright." In adult life, however, waiting a few seconds and thinking before you answer are signs of real maturity.

A mistake made in haste is regretted in leisure.

Don't eat the bitter fruit of haste.

There Are No Such Things as Opportunities Without Problems ... or Problems Without Opportunities

Charles wrote a book about his college professor. As soon as the book was published, I met Arthur, a classmate of the author, who exclaimed, "Charles wrote a book about our teacher!? There were 20 of us in class with him who were better suited and more qualified to write such a book."

Besides the "sour grapes" aspect of Arthur's

remarks, his statements ignore a basic fact. The "opportunity" to write the book came replete with many problems which Arthur and the other 19 classmates would not have wanted to solve!

What Arthur meant to say was, "If writing a book were easy and there were no problems connected with doing so, then any one of us could have done it." But the fact is that every opportunity comes with problems!

And the other side of the coin is that every problem offers us an opportunity. Soiled bandages were a major problem, but to Johnson and Johnson they provided an opportunity to invent Band-Aids. Dirty drinking glasses resulted in a health hazard ... but to Lilly they provided an opportunity to invent the paper cup.

There is an old saying that the way to success is to "find a need and fill it." The need is the problem. Identify a problem, fix it, and you have your opportunity.

You Wouldn't Be So Concerned About "What They Really Think About You" if You Realized How Seldom They Do

An infant in his crib thinks that the entire universe revolves around him. He thinks that when he goes to sleep, the universe stops.

As we grow up, we begin to realize that we are not the center of the universe and that life go on without us.

Yet many people contort their lives to meet the imagined expectations of others. They wear clothing, drive cars, build homes, and take vacations with one eye on, "What do they think of me?" and, "What will they say?" What a waste!

The truth? They won't say anything!

The "Joneses" don't think.

You Don't Fail When You Fall Unless You Fail to Get Up

How many times does it take to learn how to _____?

The right answer: as many times as it takes!

A child learning to walk is a good example of the learning/failure process. The child falls many times. Because we know that a healthy child will learn how to walk, when he does take a step we offer positive encouragement (yea! wow! great! let's call grandma!). No wonder he learns to walk in spite of the dozens of times he falls down.

We need two guiding principles:

(1) To know that we will succeed, and

(2) To get positive feedback (even if we have to give it to ourselves).

Don't Worry About What Is Ahead — Just Go as Far as You Can See Now, and From There You Will Be Able to See Further

Can you imagine someone who wants to drive across town but refuses to start until all the traffic lights are green?

Our reaction to him would be: Start now, and as you drive, the lights that are now red will turn green. If you wait for all the traffic lights to turn green you'll never move.

If we wait for the "perfect time" or "perfect situation" we can wait years.

Over the past 40 years a major organization conducted four building campaigns. In every case no sooner was the campaign announced than an earth shattering event took place: A war in Israel, an oil crisis, a drastic drop in the market ... and cries of "Now is the worst time to start a buiding campaign" were heard. "Wait for the 'Right Time.'"

Yet, the campaign continued, and the buildings were built.

Man Counts the Seeds of a Fruit. The A-mighty Counts the Fruits of a Seed.

We can see only what is in front of us. We see a fruit, and we can count the seeds.

The A-mighty sees not only the seeds in the fruit, but also every fruit that will come forth from every seed for generations.

We are told that every deed a person does has a ripple effect on other people. Thus their good actions are the continuations of the initial good deed.

When an accomplished person behaves in a way that validates the standards of conduct he has received from his parents and grandparents, it is the orchards of his forebears' seeds that are continuing to come to fruition.

We Don't See Things as They Are: We See Things as We Are

One of our greatest shortcomings is our inability to see things objectively. All of us view life from our own perspective, and we see quite subjectively: We see things *as we are*.

How do you compensate for this shortcoming? By getting second and third opinions from objective individuals and by listening carefully to these opinions, you can overcome your subjectivity. Be careful not to hear only what you want to hear. Be sure to listen to the "buts" and "maybes." They are usually the clue to what the other person *really* wants to convey without hurting your feelings.

Often the real message lies in the subtleties.

We Judge Others by Their Actions, but We Want Others to Judge Us by Our Intentions

You are a teacher, and one morning you wake up with a headache and feel feverish. You really want to take the day off and stay in bed, but because you know that an adequate substitute will not be found, you decide to go to school. You become a hero and "sacrifice" yourself for the good of your class.

When the bell signals the end of recess, you

decide to allow your class an extra 15 minutes of play. After all, you deserve to pamper yourself.

Another teacher sees you and your class enjoying the extra recess time. He is annoyed because his class feels cheated out of extra recess and blames him. You know that your intentions are honorable — even heroic — and you really want him to judge you accordingly.

But since no one can read your mind and no one can understand your intentions, you discover that people judge you only by your actions.

So we have two opposite sides of the same coin. *We* judge others by their *actions*, but we want others to judge us by our *intentions*.

Most of the Trouble in the World Is Caused by People Who Want to Be Important

Who goes first? Where will I sit? Where will my name appear? Will I get credit for the idea? Verbalized or not, these are the questions that seem most often to be on many minds.

There is no end to the limits to which a person will go to make sure he gets the credit, to push his name to the forefront — even to the point of undermining a project or torpedoing a program (there are even books and articles encouraging readers to do so because these credits might advance them in their careers!).

But these people are missing the point.

Do you know what good PR (public relations) is? The best definition of PR consists of a simple two-step program:

(1) Doing a great job, and

(2) Making sure that the right people know about it.

The fascinating thing is that "the right people" almost intuitively know precisely who does what. Such PR doesn't require pushing, shoving, or even insisting. Most often, the person's work is his or her own best salesman.

My Most Embarrassing Moments Occur When I Am Talking Instead of Listening

Either because I think I know it all or because I want to show off, I don't have the patience to listen.

Listening requires a measure of humility (perhaps someone knows more than I do), openness, and patience.

Good listening will save you much embarrassment, and you may learn a lot in the process — which means that next time you may have something really *worthwhile* to say!

The Joy of Your Excellent Proofreading Will Last Long After Your Speed Has Been Forgotten

Doing a task quickly has its benefits, but not if it is done at the expense of the quality of the work.

Think of a house painter who "quickly" paints a room in your home, but does an inferior job — or a gardener who "quickly" plants shrubbery, but not symmetrically. Every time you look at the results, instead of the joy and satisfaction that a job well done would have brought you, you will be reminded of inferior, slipshod work.

Speed is important, but not at the expense of quality.

Courage Is Going From Failure to Failure With Enthusiasm

If we learn from each new failure, we can justify the continued undertaking of new projects and ventures, notwithstanding previous failures.

Some of the world's greatest writers accumulated dozens of rejection letters before they sold their first story. In fact, one author made a game of it, to see if he could fully cover a wall in his library with rejection slips.

He sold his book just as the rejection slips were nearing the end of the wall!

Enthusiasm and courage eventually do pay off.

A Person's Enthusiasm Stands in Direct Proportion to What He Is Looking Forward To

Enthusiasm is the energy that gives power to ideas — to change, to move, and to build.

Generating this enthusiasm is, to a large extent, dependent upon one's goals.

The bigger the goal — the more grandiose it is — the more exciting it is, and the more enthusiasm it generates. Likewise, the greater the enthusiasm, the greater the chances of success, and the greater such success will be.

People Form Habits ... and Then Habits Form People

King Solomon tells us that habits are like threads. Single threads can easily be torn, but as soon as you braid several threads together, they become as strong as a heavy rope.

To do something once or twice may seem innocent enough, but we never know at which point these actions become habits. And a habit is very hard to break.

And that's great ... because by doing good things several times we can create "good habits"! Good action habits (for example, doing certain *mitzvos*, coming on time, and being pleasant) and good thought habits (such as thinking kindly about people and giving people the benefit of the doubt) are the character builders from which we all can profit!

Life Has Not Taken Hold of You Until You Begin Doing Things That the Average Person Considers Impossible

What does the phrase "life taking hold of you" mean to you? It may mean changing your thinking from "just surviving" to "thriving"! There is a rush of adrenaline and a pounding of the heart that come from challenges. Can I really do this? Is this project too big for me? Can I introduce a new product? Can I learn a new discipline? At my age can I undertake something new?

A goal that people believe to be "impossible" can be the right challenge to ignite the enthusiasm of a positive, confident person. Big goals and big dreams (that most people say are impossible) can really turn you on.

During World War II, this was the motto of the Seabees, the U.S. Navy Corps of Engineers: "The hard jobs we do right away. The impossible ones take a little longer."

It Is Easier for Most People to Adjust Themselves to the Hardships Involved in Making a Poor Living Than to Adjust Themselves to the Hardships Involved in Making Their Lives Better

Man is capable of adjusting to various and sundry new and even difficult situations. If it were not for this ability, a person would not be able to tolerate discomfort. As a result, if the weather is too hot or too cold, a seat too hard, or a bed too soft, a person can learn to tolerate these and many other circumstances.

People have survived severe hardships and physical and emotional pain for years and even decades because of their ability to tolerate them.

Yet this very ability to tolerate has a down side. A person can find himself in a bad situation with the means to improve, but he may choose instead to tolerate it.

Be careful. What you get used to may stop you from wanting to improve your circumstances.

NEVER BE A SLAVE TO THE TYRANNY OF THE URGENT

We must have it *immediately*.

It is urgent.

It is an *emergency*!

Sometimes it is; most often (unless you are a doctor in an emergency room), it is not.

Demands generated by businesses and even by family members have so increased that an immediate reply by e-mail is expected within seconds.

But for the most part, it does not have to be

that way. You can choose *not* to be a slave to the urgent, not to play the game of the "now" and "immediate" generation.

Don't forget. Immediacy is the enemy of reflection — and reflection is the mother of success.

To Be Successful, We Don't Have to Find Something New; We Need Only to Find Ways of Doing Old Things Better

We are constantly amazed at how much better something can be done. You work in an office where some procedures have been improved over the years to the point that you would think they could not be improved upon any further.

Then a new employee comes in and suggests an even better way to do it!

We need to remember that improvement has (almost) no limits, and that we must constantly question whether or not there might be a better way to do something — and we must certainly be open to suggestions.

That "better way" can open the door to new opportunities.

IF EXCELLENCE IS MY GOAL, THEN CRITICISM IS MY ALLY

Because criticism touches the very essence of a person — his ego — he is supersensitive to it. Yet if understood objectively, criticism is a tool to facilitate improvement — and a very powerful tool at that.

Imagine two people who begin working in a company at the same time, each possessing approximately the same skills. The first employee takes criticism personally. When his supervisor makes a comment, he tries to justify himself or begrudgingly accepts these suggestions as though they were imposed upon him.

The second employee is open to criticism: He welcomes it and readily accepts it. After being criticized about one of his actions, he tries to improve, making a point of showing his new effort to his supervisor and asking him whether the earlier error has now been corrected.

Which employee do you think will advance faster — and which employee will have greater opportunities in this company?

Children (and adults as well) have to be taught and shown that criticism is not a form of depreciation. It is perhaps the single most powerful tool for personal growth.

Thoughts about more- and less-effective ways to criticize children:

Less Effective:
- In public

- In anger
- Loudly
- Negatively
- Randomly
- The more the better
- Reminding of past errors

More Effective:
- In private
- With love
- Softly
- Positively
- Selectively
- The least bit necessary
- Inspiring future accomplishments

Don't Depend on Anyone Else for Your Happiness, for Your Fulfillment, or for Your Growth

"**H**e or she is responsible to make me happy" is an attitude that can spell trouble for any relationship. The unvarnished truth is that you — and only you — are responsible for your happiness, or better said, only you can make yourself happy or unhappy.

The very same applies to fulfillment and growth. Follow the development of a child. As a child, a young boy or girl is given an "educational program" (commonly known as school) designed to systematically provide him or her with continuing education. As the youngster grows up and completes his formal schooling, he learns that there is no one to show him the next step. He finds a job or enters a career and finds himself waiting for someone to provide him with a plan for his continuing education. He can wait for years and decades to no avail until he realizes that he — and only he — is responsible for himself!

This ideal may seem simple and axiomatic, yet the vast majority of people don't understand it. Many people expect someone — a boss, employer, supervisor, principal, sales-manager, or even a spouse — to provide a "curriculum for personal growth." But this just isn't so! At best, they may help you, but the bottom line is that you and you alone are responsible for your happiness, fulfillment, and growth.

FOR THE PERSON WHO IS WILLING TO SERVE BEFORE TRYING TO COLLECT ... THERE ARE ABUNDANT OPPORTUNITIES

One of the great lessons that every child who grew up on a farm intuitively knew, was that first you have to plant, then you can expect to harvest.

Our society with its "buy now, pay later" mentality teaches an unrealistic lesson that not only effects credit card purchases but also an attitude towards many areas in life.

"When they pay me more, then I'll work better" is an example of this philosophy in the work place ... but it just flaunts the way real life operates.

The interesting thing is that your employer does not control the sort of service you render.

You and only you control that, and it is the major factor that can make or break you.

A Great Deal of Talent Is Lost to the World for Want of Courage. Talent Resides in Action.

We all know extremely talented people who have gotten nowhere despite their talent because they failed to take action.

Taking action takes courage. Until you do something, you are not wrong. The minute you take action, you risk being wrong; you risk being laughed at.

On the other hand, a person who has less talent, but takes risks, makes mistakes, and learns from these mistakes will go on to succeed.

The person who never fails never grows. When success comes, the failures are forgotten or become subjects for good-natured laughter.

People Grow Old by Deserting Their Ideals

You are as young as your faith and as old as your doubt; as young as your self-confidence and as old as your fear; as young as your hopes and as old as your despair.

Age is a technical function of the clock and calendar. "Growing old," however, is a concept usually described by words such as "used-up," "spent," "stale," and "decrepit."

The fact is that there are men and women well into their 70's, 80's, and even 90's who are vibrant, exciting, fresh, and enthusiastic about life.

What do you imagine to be a major factor in why one person is old and spent, while another is vibrant and enthusiastic?

Surprisingly, health, family, and financial independence are relatively minor factors. The major difference is whether or not a person feels that he has an overriding reason to live and a goal to achieve!

BE HAPPY WITH WHAT YOU HAVE WHILE IN PURSUIT OF WHAT YOU WANT

We all know: "Who is rich? He who is happy with what he has." But if you're really happy with what you have, will that prevent you from advancing?

Not necessarily. There are two separate steps that you could take:

(1) Be happy with what you have. You have the ability to be happy now with whatever has been granted you. And at the same time,

(2) You can pursue the improvement, the amelioration of your situation.

You show that you are happy with what you have by expressing thankfulness and by not complaining. You smile and you are pleasant.

You pursue improvement by setting aside time every day to master new skills or to do whatever it takes to better your situation. These are two separate concepts — to be happy with what you have and to pursue improvement. They are different but not contradictory. By buying into both, you will live contentedly now and — even more so — in the future.

What I Am to Be, I Am Now Becoming

There is no "secret formula" to take, no "magic button" to push, to enable you to become the person you want to be.

It is simply a process of doing each day that which will help you to become that person.

One should ask himself a very simple question daily: Is what I am doing now moving me closer to any of my goals?

HEALTHY RELATIONSHIPS ARE USUALLY SWEET-TEMPERED

Even when it is necessary to firmly refuse a request, your refusal can be sweet-tempered.

You have been asked to do something that you can't do at this time. The right answer is "No!" But there are many ways to say "No." One extreme might be a cold indignant "No!" that implies, "It's your problem; I couldn't care less!" On the other hand, it could be, "No, I can't do it at this time, but perhaps we can spend just a few minutes to think of other ways in which you can get what you need."

A friend had the unpleasant job of firing an employee. He agonized about it for a few days and finally developed a strategy to present it in the most positive light. The employee was obviously upset, but because the manner in which it was presented was "sweet-tempered," they remained friends.

DID YOU DO YOUR BEST? IF NOT, WHY NOT?

These two questions should be asked at the completion of every task.

"Did you do your best?" intends to measure the person against himself, his abilities, and his skills. It says, "You're in competition with only yourself."

The second question simply asks, "If not, why not?" If you haven't done your best, what is your reason for not having done so? You evaluate the honesty and validity of your excuse.

These are two powerful questions that can help you grow. Did you do your best? If not, why not?

Perhaps My Life's Challenge Is to Be Humble Even When I'm Right (to Compensate for My Being Arrogant When I Am Wrong)

That seems to be my challenge. Each of us has his or her own challenge regarding the improvement of a character trait. Usually the challenge is the trait that is most difficult for him or her to improve upon.

For a shy person, the challenge is not to control himself to be quiet: After all, he is naturally taciturn. His challenge is to speak up when necessary.

For a person who can't stop talking, the challenge is not to speak: His challenge is to learn when to be silent.

THE POWER OF THREE-WORD PHRASES

There are phrases that in just a few words convey a whole attitude. In fact, when it comes to words, instead of "more is better" the truth is "less is better." Following are six such three-word power phrases.

(1) *It's my baby.* I once asked a successful fundraiser what quality he looked for in choosing a chairperson for a project. He told me that to him the most important quality was to find a person who felt, "It's my baby."

When the proud parents bring home their

cute, lovable baby from the hospital, they make a commitment to love and care for that baby at all times and in all circumstances. It's easy to do this when the baby is cute, clean, and cuddly; but because he or she is *their baby*, the commitment is there even when the baby is dirty and crying. Even if the baby is not well and is up the whole night, the parents' love and concern remain unchanged.

These words say, "I will see it through all problems, even when the going gets rough."

There is magic in commitment. It says, "I'm in it for the long run; you can count on me," and "I'm not going to be scared away by problems."

(2) *Whatever it takes*. Similar to the commitment of "It's my baby," this phrase expresses a deep commitment to the successful completion of a project.

The story is told of a sculptor in Mexico who — in the midst of working on a major sculpture — had an unfortunate, freak accident that cost him the use of his right hand, the hand that he used for work.

After a period of hospitalization and recovery, he regained his composure and became determined to complete the sculpture. He taught himself how to work with his left hand, and months later he completed his sculpture. He named his work, "In spite of ..."

That's the level of "whatever it takes" that we are talking about.

(3) *I'll handle it.* The diametric opposite of "It's not my job," this phrase, "I'll handle it," says that it's under my control and that I'll take care of all the details, all the paper work, and all the phone calls — the whole thing.

A friend told me the following story. He had rented out his home. Accidentally, a small child broke the plastic shelf on the inside panel of the refrigerator door. The woman who rented the home said, "I'll handle it," and did the following:

(a) After making six phone calls, she found the craftsman who would install the part if she was able to get it.

(b) After making four calls and working her way through tens of "telephone menus," and being put on hold many times, she reached the manufacturer and ordered the replacement panel.

(c) She arranged for the craftsman to come to the house at the most convenient time to install the new panel.

(d) After the installation, she came to check on the job and remove all the packing material.

My friend was left with no loose ends, no mess to clean, and no bills to pay. Nothing. The woman handled it entirely.

Compare this woman with someone who does some part of a project but assumes that someone else will be there to complete it.

How refreshing it is when the words "I'll

handle it" are followed up by appropriate action.

(4) *Seize the moment.* All we have is today. Yesterday is history, tomorrow is but a promise. Today is all we have at our disposal. Teach yourself to seize the moment. Do all you can now, with what you have now.

(5) *It's no problem.* This phrase has unfortunately become an overused, easily spoken "throwaway" to the point that it has become meaningless. But when it is meant, the person who says "It's no problem" in answer to a request is really saying that he or she views your request as a challenge — not as a problem — and will comply to the best of his or her ability.

(6) *It's my fault.* Personal responsibility is one of the major criteria of maturity. The child says, "It broke." The adult says, "I broke it." Only someone who is willing to accept personal responsibility can progress to correct his behavior.

The Mistake We Often Make Is That We Stop Working on Ourselves as Soon as We Are Doing Better

It happens in many areas. The salesman who is in a selling slump reads several sales-improvement books and starts to do better — and immediately stops his reading.

The person who feels weak starts an exercise program, feels better, and abruptly stops his exercise program. The real challenge is to continue working on ourselves, systematically improving even after we have started to feel better. Since at this point most people stop improving, the person who *does* continue to advance will grow to be head-and-shoulders above everyone else.

IF YOU DON'T APPRECIATE YOUR STRENGTHS, YOU CAN'T ELIMINATE YOUR WEAKNESSES

To honestly know oneself — in terms of both strengths and weaknesses — is truly a blessing.

Some people deny their strengths (they mistakenly think that this is a sign of humility, or they may be afraid of failure); others deny their weaknesses (they mistakenly think that by admitting to a weakness they are less of a person).

Knowing your strong points enables you to capitalize and build on them. Knowing your weaknesses allows you to develop programs to strengthen them.

What You Take for Granted, Your Children Don't Even Know

Closing a light when you leave a room, writing a thank-you note, not eating while standing, replacing your chair after you eat, and hundreds of such simple basic conventions *need to be taught* to children.

There was a time that we took it for granted that a child growing up in a home would absorb all his elders' manners and life skills through osmosis.

Today, it is just not so. Perhaps because parents are more permissive, or because they spend less intimate time with their children, or because of the influence of the media, children just don't pick up those behaviors by themselves. What a parent or teacher would have considered elementary and unnecessary to discuss several decades ago, today needs to be *taught*!

Until your child demonstrates to you that he does know and has internalized these social skills, you can't assume that he is even aware of them.

What You Consider a Well-deserved Luxury, Your Children Deem a Necessity

Both parents worked hard for the first 30 years of marriage: They spent conservatively, saved carefully, and invested wisely. They rarely took vacations and drove a 12-year-old car.

Now after 30 years of scrimping, their financial situation has improved, and they decide to treat themselves to a better car, not the top-of-the-line model, but one that is extremely comfortable and luxurious.

In a few short months, there is a subtle but noticeable change in the attitude of the children still living at home. Driving a new car is the only way to go, they think. They don't realize that this luxury was earned through a lifetime of hard work, and they assume that they too deserve a new car. It has become a necessity to them; the fact that their parents earned the right to own one is lost on them.

Think back to your own childhood, and remember what was a luxury to your parents and what you convinced yourself was an indispensable necessity. Now apply this scenario today to your own children!

Here are two considerations:

(a) Give serious thought before you treat yourself to even well-deserved luxuries. Consider their far-reaching impact on your present way of life.

(b) Discuss with your family the fact that

these luxuries have come after a lifetime of modest living.

(Note: In truth, consideration "b" really doesn't work very well; "a" is much more effective.)

Don't Buy a "Bargain in Reverse"

A shortcut is often the quickest way to some place you weren't going. Shortcuts and bargains share the same attraction — the opportunity to get something for almost nothing.

Every day, people take shortcuts and get lost in places where they never should have been in the first place, and buy "bargains" they don't need, don't have place to store, and can't use!

A friend told me the following story. He was working for a non-profit organization, and someone donated an old addressing machine. This monstrous machine required a special trucking company to haul it (but it was a bargain!). The organization had to convert their mailing list to 14,000 metal address plates at 10 cents apiece (but we got the machine for nothing!), several visits from a repairman (you have to expect an old machine to need some overhauling, but don't worry — it was still a bargain!), and finally after several frustrating months, a junk man was paid to haul it away (but it was a great bargain!).

What a beautiful example of a "bargain in reverse"!

Don't Write — Rewrite

Next time you or someone else close to you says, "I'm not a writer" or, "I can't write," tell him that the vast majority of written material — books, magazines, and articles — has been written by people who *rewrite*. Few writers, even the most professional ones, are capable of producing a quality written piece the first time.

What they do — and what you can easily learn to do — is to put down their thoughts on paper as quickly as possible. At the first writing, ignore structure, choice of words, grammar, and spelling. All you want to do is to get the thoughts flowing. Then you have time to rewrite your first draft a second, third, and fourth time — or as many times as it takes. In each revision, you will attempt to make the thoughts clearer and more precise, use richer language, and correct the grammar.

You can ask two friends to read your work to see if they understand the points you're making. Then rewrite your article again to reflect their comments, and repeat the process.

You would be surprised to know how many times even seemingly simple paragraphs are rewritten — and, using this method, how many non-professionals have written well. Don't write — rewrite!

Success Principle: Under-Promise And Over-Deliver

We are so accustomed to people who over-promise and under-deliver that when we meet a person who just keeps his word we are delighted.

When someone exceeds his promises, we are overwhelmed.

- We like such a person.
- We want him as our friend.
- We want to do business with such a person.

This is a simple but powerful method to achieve success.

Don't Ask, "What Will I Get?" Rather Ask, "What Will I Become?"

The first question most people ask when they apply for a job is, "What will I get?" Granted, the major reason for working is to earn money, but we can't be oblivious to the fact that in addition to earning money, our personalities are influenced by the type of business in which we are employed and even more, by the people with whom we are in daily contact.

To work in the office of an exciting entrepreneur who is supportive and encouraging may be worth much more than the extra money you can earn in an office where people are negative, secretive, and self-serving, or complacent and resistant to change.

After a few years of close association, you will probably take on some of the characteristics of your colleagues. Observe them carefully *now*, to see whether in the future you want to look and act like them.

SUCCESS COMES TO THOSE WHO REFUSE TO FAIL

If you read the biographies of people who have achieved something of great value in their lifetimes, you will notice that almost every one of them faced a crisis that threatened to prevent him from continuing, a threat so huge that it imperiled the very existence of the project to which he had dedicated years!

We're talking about debilitating illness, the death of a spouse, bankruptcy, political disfavor with the ruling government — really major challenges!

In almost every situation, a person on the way to doing something great had many *justified* reasons for quitting. Working for years on a manuscript, only to watch the only copy go up in flames, is certainly a reason for anyone to say, "I've had it." Climbing a mountain, then watching your comrades fall to their deaths, is enough reason to quit before reaching the summit. But these people didn't quit.

You may not have to face such dramatic challenges. But even in your work, there are always "justified" reasons to quit: "I tried, and it didn't work"; "It was the wrong time"; "I wasn't up to it"; "I'm waiting for the right time" — we frequently hear these alibis.

Consider this: Effort fully releases its reward *only after a person refuses to quit!*

There Is No Glory in the Preparation to Win, but You Can't Have the Glory of the "Win" Without the Preparation

Winning brings glory. It brings glamour, excitement, public acclaim, very often financial rewards, and always deep personal satisfaction!

The *preparation* to win has none of these. By nature, it is lonely, hard, unglamorous, dull, repetitious, and tedious. It deprives you of fun;

you have to sacrifice your time, effort, and money. But you can't have the "win" without the preparation for the win.

A speaker inspires an audience in a short 20-minute speech. You don't know that his presentation was the result of six boring hours of practice.

You are impressed by the clarity of thought in a short article. You don't know that the author has labored tens of tedious hours rewriting it.

Indeed, the clergyman, lecturer, doctor, lawyer, artist, athlete, craftsman, or other professional has spent hours, days, and weeks in monotonous, unexciting preparation before dazzling us with his brilliant "win."

I Don't Eat Junk Food Because I Need My Body to Perform at Its Best so That I Can Perform at My Best

Doing our best takes physical effort. When we are functioning at our physical optimum, we can hope to produce at a high level. While there are so many illnesses and physical limitations beyond our control, eating good food — providing our bodies with maximum nutrition — is within our ability.

When we eat junk food place in place of nutritious food, we are deliberately weakening our ability and performance.

A race horse is fed only the most nourishing feed because his trainer clearly understands the relationship between food input and energy output. Yet the horse's owner stuffs his own body with junk foods, the kinds he would never feed his horse!

There Is No Sadder Sight Than A Young Pessimist

The same is true of a young cynic! Youth is the time to dream big, bold dreams and to believe in doing the impossible.

As people grow older, life's hardships temper these dreams. If a young person starts out with pessimism in place of optimism, when he grows older he will have amassed a litany of hundreds of reasons why "I couldn't do it." The optimist will be able to add just one comment: "But I did it."

Pessimism is gray hair on a young man's head.

You Steer a Sailboat by Adjusting Its Rudders

You steer a sailboat by adjusting its rudders hundreds of times every hour. If each time you have to make a change you consider it a failure, you're doomed. However, if each change is perceived as an adjustment, you'll reach your destination.

You are on a beautiful lake, a nice wind at your back — the perfect condition for sailing in a straight line from point A to point B.

But you never do go in a straight line! The wind changes direction and velocity ever so slightly every few seconds; every passing boat creates a wake that rocks your boat. It is only your constant adjustment of the rudder (and sails) that gets you to your destination.

How do you perceive change? Is it failure or adjustment? Life is like sailing a boat. We want to go to our destination — success in terms of good health, loving family, adhering to our beliefs, reaching our financial goals, and being socially prominent — and yet we are constantly obligated to adjust our course to stay on course.

How do you perceive change — as a failure or as a necessary adjustment?

Most of the Progress Made by a Sailboat Is Against the Wind

Most people think that a sailboat proceeds by being pushed directly by the wind blowing from behind the boat. That is true only 20 percent of the time. In 80 percent of the time the winds are not coming directly from the back but from one side. It is up to the skill of the sailor to adjust the sail to take advantage of the wind, and head the boat in the direction he wants to sail.

You can observe a lake with the wind blowing from one direction and, nevertheless, sailboats are sailing in all different directions — being propelled by the same wind!

Life is similar. It's not what happens that determines our direction, but rather what we do with what happens that determines our direction.

The Effectiveness of a Sailboat Is in the Coordination of the sail and the Rudder

A sailboat has two major components: a sail to catch the wind and provide the power for movement, and a rudder to give direction to the boat.

The sailboat will sail optimally — smoothly, quickly, and efficiently — when the sail and rudder are perfectly coordinated. This may require one to make minute adjustments to both the angle of the sail and the position of the rudder many times.

To the casual observer, the sail high in the wind, and the rudder deep in the water have little in common. Yet, every sailor knows that it is only the perfect harmony between these two that will make for great sailing. Only when he positions the sail and rudder to head the boat in the same direction will the boat provide a safe and pleasant trip.

How similar this is to the family. The husband and wife each have totally different functions; but it is only the coordination between them — the heading in the same direction — that can create a pleasant climate, one that will nurture wholesome growth.

Although There Is Never Enough Time to Do Everything, There Is Always Enough Time to Do the Most Important Thing — and to Stay With It Until It Is Done Right

"**I** don't have the time" has become part of our language. What it really means is that I have given a higher priority to other things for which I *do* have time, and I therefore don't have enough time to spare for this particular task.

Have you ever seen someone who does not have the time to sit down for even a moment but talks for a half an hour before leaving for some seemingly urgent appointment?

Make sure that the really important things in your life get their needed time.

Don't Just Go Through Life: Grow Through It!

We're all going to go through life in one way or another. Why not make it through by growing in every area?

Can you look back to the last year or to five years ago and point to those areas where you are now better, more learned, more advanced, or more skilled?

In one year or five years from today, in which way will you be better — more learned, more advanced, or more skilled? What is your plan?

Ask for Help — not Because You Are Weak, but Because You Want to Remain Strong

A couple is driving through an unfamiliar city and are lost. The wife suggests that they ask for directions. The husband refuses because he perceives asking for directions as a sign of weakness. He reasons that "a real man can figure it out."

He is willing to travel miles in the wrong direction and arrive late to his destination to uphold his misguided perception!

Refusing to ask for help in finding an address is one of life's minor problems. Refusing to ask for direction in areas of health, religious practice, choice of career, marriage, and child rearing, on the other hand, is a *major* mistake.

Don't allow your wrong perception to keep you from seeking the right direction.

Until the Pain of Staying the Same Is Greater Than the Pain of Change, We Will Never Change

What does the phrase "the pain of change" mean to you? Is there really "pain" in change?

To many people, just the *thought* of change is enough to create pain. It makes them feel inadequate.

There are thousands of men and women who are so afraid of change that they would rather suffer the life of a widow or widower than consider the change of remarriage. They would rather stay in dead-end jobs than risk the pain of change to a different career.

The irony is that in many situations the "pain" of change is an illusion. Yet we allow this fear to control and restrict our lives.

Refusing to Accept Things as They Are Is What Drives a Person To Great Accomplishments

As children and then as students we are taught: Just do it. Don't question, don't ask, don't improve: Just do it.

Although there are times, ages, and places for such thinking, there are also many situations in which being dissatisfied and doing something about the source of this dissatisfaction can lead to major improvements.

Just imagine how many people tolerated endless traffic jams because they resisted the idea of one-way streets. Think about how many people tolerated parking their cars to make one-minute bank deposits until someone thought of drive-thru banking.

The test of dissatisfaction is this: *To what does it lead?* If being dissatisfied means only endless complaints and frustration, it doesn't do anything for anyone.

If, however, dissatisfaction inspires a person to want to change and to begin the process of change, it then becomes a great motivator.

On The Average, Each Person Will Experience (Either He Himself Or Someone Close To Him) Several Major Tragedies

Expect them.

Brace yourself for them.

Handle them.

Problems: Either You Just Left One, or You Are in One, or You Are Headed Toward One

Tension is what gives a bow the power to propel an arrow. If there is minimal tension, the arrow receives little energy from the bow. If, however, there is too much tension, the archer will be unable to transfer energy from the bow to the arrow.

Problems to a person are similar to tension in a bow.

If we could create a problem-free state, we would lack the propellant to move us forward and upward. We would become complacent and fat.

Therefore, our attitude toward "problems" should be that problems (or, better said, "challenges") are the method by which we are propelled forward. We may not understand the reason why this is so, or necessarily appreciate the challenges, but they are part and parcel of life.

Just When You See the Light at the End of the Tunnel, They Add More Tunnel

Or so it seems. Just as we're about to solve one problem, new ones appear.

Those who look for a perfect state of affairs without problems — where things always work right, people always keep promises, and schedules are always met — will invariably be disappointed.

Folk wisdom puts it this way: "Just as soon as a mother thinks her work is finished, she becomes a grandmother."

No Blame. No Excuses. No Complaints. No Self-Pity.

Can you imagine visiting a hospital for the chronically ill and meeting a 38-year-old patient? He has spent the last eight years in this hospital and will probably spend the foreseeable future in similar institutions.

On the wall you spot a small frame with a crude hand-printed inscription containing just the eight words listed above. In your conversation you ask him what the story behind these phrases is. He tells you that in that frame is his life's credo. He adopted it many years ago when he first became sick. At that time he was angry, bitter, and resentful. After much thought, reading, and prayer, he adopted the four phrases as his credo, and his life subsequently became more tolerable and then pleasant; now he is fully content. The hospital staff loves him. Friends visit him constantly. He is a pleasure to be with.

IF YOU'RE NOT ACTIVELY INVOLVED IN GETTING WHAT YOU WANT, YOU DON'T REALLY WANT IT ENOUGH

You would be surprised at how many people fool themselves for years with the words, "When I have the time, I will ..."

A good test of how you might use your retirement time for a planned project is to see how much time you give it while you are still gainfully employed.

A Wise Man Demands of Himself What a Fool Demands of Others

We have no problem in seeing even the smallest fault in others and in demanding that they adhere to a high standard, but we often fail to see similar faults in ourselves.

A wise man makes great demands of himself. He wants to meet his own criteria. He wants to see whether he can outdo his own record of achievements.

A Wise Man Learns From His Mistakes. A Wiser Man Learns From Mistakes Made by Others.

There is no doubt that experience is the best teacher. But must it necessarily be *your own* experience? Must you personally taste the spoiled milk once others have told you that it is sour? Must you personally experience the pain of touching a hot stove after you have seen how others have been burned?

Life is too short and the risks are too high for

you to have to personally experience the failures and mistakes of others.

Experience is the best teacher, but learning from the experience of others is an even better teacher.

About the Author

Mr. Avi Shulman was a classroom teacher for over 25 years, National Director of Torah Umesorah's S.E.E.D. program, and currently teaches in Aish Dos and Mercaz Teacher Training Programs.

He is the author of 20 personal growth and parenting books and cassette programs, and writes a popular weekly column for Torah Umesorah published in the Yated Ne'eman.

Mr. Shulman is a nationally acclaimed speaker and teacher.